Mwanza FLYING HIGH as a PILOT

by Charlotte Rolfe and Mwanza Lombanya

MACMILLAN

First published 2001 by
MACMILLAN EDUCATION LTD
London and Oxford
Companies and representatives throughout the world

ISBN 0–333–92451–7

10	9	8	7	6	5	4	3	2	1
10	09	08	07	06	05	04	03	02	01

This book is printed on paper suitable for recycling and
made from fully managed and sustained forest sources.

Printed in China

A catalogue record for this book is available from the British Library.

Acknowledgements
The authors and publishers wish to acknowledge, with thanks, the following
photographic sources:
Corel Corporation p2 above, p7 below, p21 below; Magic Carpet Advertising and
Promotions, Zambia, title page; Panos p2 below right, p3 above left; Rex Features
p2 below left; Robson Syankamu p4 above; Zambia Information Services p3
above right and below, p12 above.

Photographs not listed above were provided by the authors.

Illustrations by Maureen and Gordon Gray; Illustrated Arts
Series design by Geoffrey Wadsley; cover by AC Design
Produced for Macmillan Education Ltd by Aldridge Press

The publishers have made every effort to trace the copyright holders, but if they
have inadvertently overlooked any, they will be pleased to make the necessary
arrangements at the first opportunity.

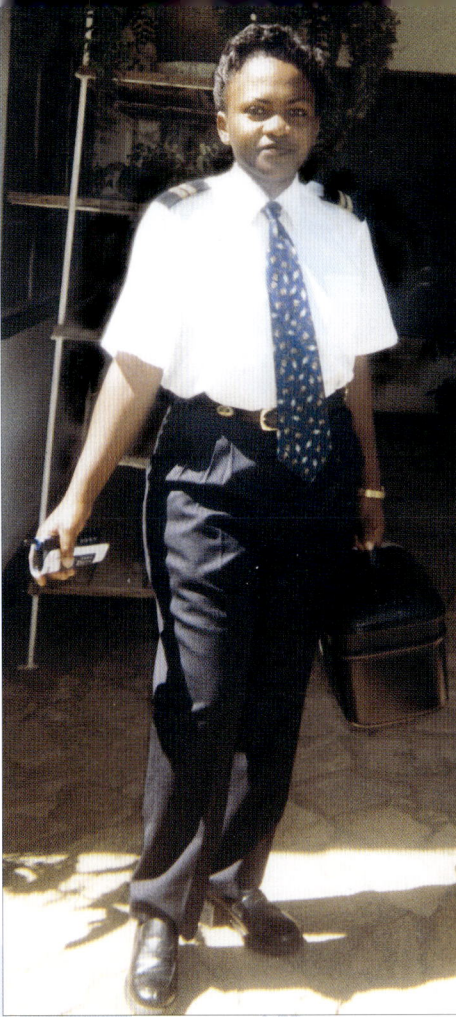

Reporting for duty

It's a bright sunny morning in Lusaka, Zambia's capital city. Mwanza is going to work. She says goodbye to her young son, Mambwe, before she leaves for Lusaka's international airport.

This morning Mwanza will be flying a passenger plane north to Kitwe, the country's second biggest city. After a twenty-minute stop at Kitwe airport, she will co-pilot the return flight to Lusaka.

In the afternoon she will be flying to Livingstone, on the Zambezi river.

What's it like to be a pilot, flying high above the wide, open spaces of central Africa? What different jobs do pilots do – and how do they learn to fly? Let's find out from Mwanza …

In the air

Mwanza loves flying. Her work as a pilot has taken her all over Zambia, and to other countries, too.

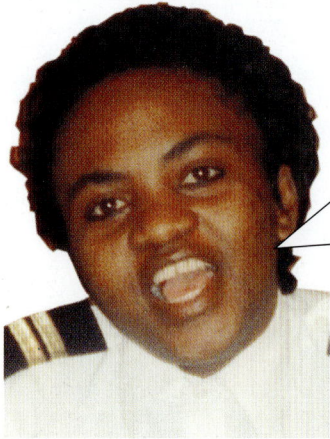

The most important thing for any pilot is to understand everything about the plane they are flying. You really have to know your plane like the back of your hand!

A Boeing 747 'Jumbo Jet' prepares for take-off. Passenger aeroplanes like these are busy all over Africa. They carry several million passengers every year.

Pilots are trained to fly different types of aircraft. On this page you can see a few of these different flying machines and the work they do.

An air rescue team at work during a flood disaster. They have spotted a woman half hidden in the trees and are preparing to lift her to safety.

This helicopter is spraying a breeding site of the oncho fly that causes river blindness in people.

A Buffalo plane lands at a rural airstrip to deliver food and medicine.

Unloading maize meal for a rural community in Zambia.

A Short Solent flying boat making a stop on the Zambezi river during the 1940s.

Did you know?

Flying boats

Some of the first aircraft to fly over Africa used the continent's big lakes and rivers as landing strips! Flying boats like the one in this picture used to fly in stages from Cairo in Egypt all the way to Cape Town in South Africa. They stopped on Lake Victoria in East Africa, and on the great Zambezi river. They had to stop quite often to take on more fuel. Gradually they were replaced by the land aircraft which we know today; these were less expensive to operate.

Early days

Mwanza was born third in a family of five children. Her parents lived and worked in Lusaka, so she grew up in the city. Their home was in Chelston, on the eastern side of Lusaka, not far from the airport.

❝With two older brothers, there was always quite a lot of competition in our family. I was encouraged to do well at school by both my parents, and I wanted my brothers to see that I could do as well as them.❞

Mwanza, aged eight, (right) with her younger sister, Mandona.

Mwanza's mother worked as a secretary and her father was a busy journalist so there were always lots of interesting stories and events to discuss at home.

❝I was quite a serious child I suppose. I used to read a lot. I shared storybooks with my best friend at primary school, and my parents encouraged me to listen to the news.❞

Mwanza's primary school was only about ten minutes' walk from her home, and she still remembers her class teacher.

4

> Miss Mundia was strict, but she was a wonderful teacher, and she gave me a strong love of learning. Even now, I need to keep up to date with new technology in modern aircraft, so I'm still learning!

At Kabulonga Girls' Secondary School, Mwanza's favourite subjects were maths and physics – her parents thought she might become a doctor. But that's not how things turned out. One school holidays, Mwanza went with her brothers to stay with a cousin and his family. He worked for Zambia's Air Force. He took the children to visit a hangar – a big building where some of the planes were kept. Mwanza was allowed to see inside one of the planes.

> I'd never been in an aeroplane before, and I sat in the pilot's seat and touched the controls. I closed my eyes and I dreamed I was flying. It was great. I didn't realise it at the time, but I think that awakened my interest in flying as a career.

Apart from doing her school studies, Mwanza also edited a school magazine called *Cozmag*. Some fellow students decided to interview Mwanza for *Cozmag*, and in the interview she admitted that she wanted to be a pilot.

> Everyone thought it was a huge joke, and I was teased about it for a long time afterwards. Nobody believed that a girl could become a pilot, especially not one who was only 1.6 metres tall! But in a way, it made me more determined.

Mwanza celebrates the end of the school year in Form Five with her friends.

Learning to fly

Mwanza completed her school education in Form Five, and found a job in a bank. But she didn't forget her dream. Soon afterwards, she saw an advertisement in the newspaper:

The Department of Technical Education and Vocational Training invites applications for the Pilot Trainee Programme at the Zambia Air Services Training Institute (ZASTI). Applicants should be Form Five graduates with good passes in Mathematics, English, Sciences and Geography. Applications, with copies of certificates, to reach us by 1st August

Mwanza couldn't wait to tell her family.

❝My parents were very understanding. They knew this was the chance I'd been waiting for. I completed the forms and sent them in, then I waited.❞

There were several thousand applicants and Mwanza knew that only ten people would be chosen. Did she have a chance?

❝I was thrilled to be called for the first interview but I still felt worried about my height. It was a big comfort later to see a young man on the course who was the same height as me!❞

The interview was challenging. All the candidates had to answer questions which tested their natural ability for flying.

❝On the personal side, I think they were looking for people with a strong sense of responsibility. Flying is all about safety. For example, it's important to complete all the checks, before, during and after every flight, no matter how small these are. And a pilot must stay calm and think clearly at all times – especially in an emergency.❞

Key skills for flying

- close attention to detail
- good hand-to-eye coordination
- confidence with maths and technical information
- good powers of observation
- general knowledge
- good health and general fitness

After the interviews and medical tests, Mwanza won a place on the course. There were eight male trainees and one other female student pilot. The first six months were spent, not in the air, but in 'ground school'.

The class of ten trainee pilots at ZASTI.

❝❝Apart from aerodynamics – learning about how things fly – we had to study a number of other subjects such as meteorology, navigation, radio operation and air law. Every pilot has to know the rules about taking off and landing, what equipment you must carry in the plane, and what you must do in an emergency.❞❞

plan. They must calculate how much fuel is needed, check directions by using flight instruments, and estimate 'wind drift' – wind affects the speed and direction of the plane.

Radio operation: Pilots use the radio to communicate with ground staff at the airport. In smaller aircraft, pilots also use the radio to pick up signals from special radio stations all over the country. These signals help pilots to navigate accurately. Through the signals, they know where they are in relation to each radio station and they can easily find their way home or to the nearest airport.

Meteorology: Every pilot needs to know about the weather. For example, these cumulus clouds often contain strong up and down air movements, known as turbulence. Turbulence makes a plane pitch and roll; a flight through these clouds will be a bumpy one!

Navigation: A pilot often has to change direction due to bad weather, so all pilots need to know how to change their flight

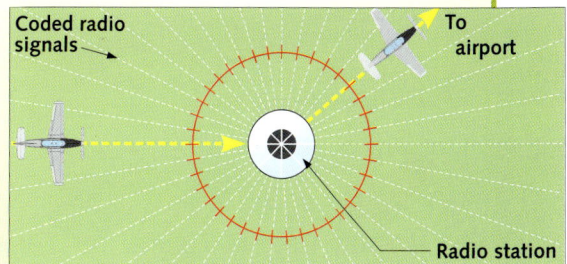

Coded radio signals

To airport

Radio station

Airborne!

Mwanza began to practise flying with the help of the school's flying instructors.

"Getting the plane up into the air and landing it smoothly are the two hardest moves for a new pilot. I learnt how to use the throttle to give the plane the right amount of engine power, but at the same time to get the angle of the plane right. It's quite easy to stall the aircraft or to go into a spin if you don't balance these two things. My instructors were very patient and helped me to get it right."

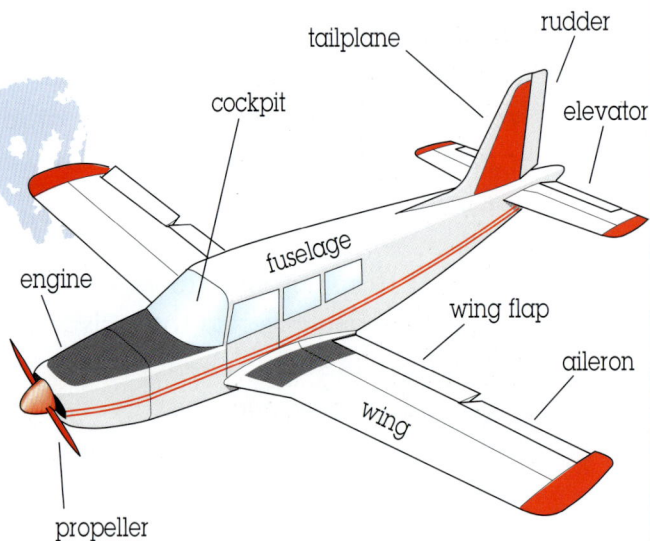

The pictures below show the four forces which act on a plane as it flies. On the page opposite, you can see some of the basic controls and how they work.

UNDERSTANDING AERODYNAMICS:
the forces which act on a plane

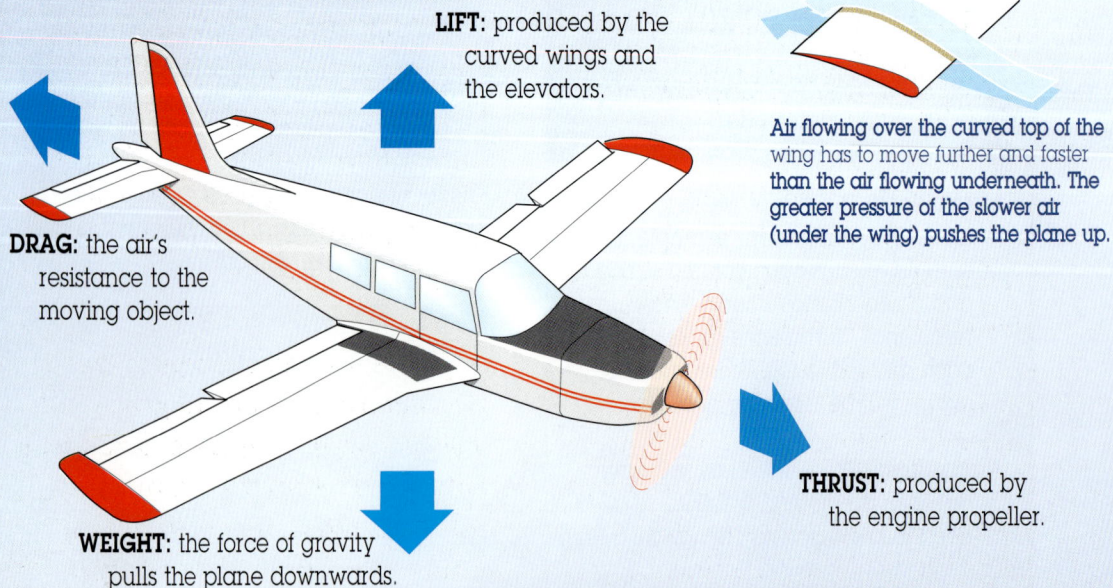

LIFT: produced by the curved wings and the elevators.

Air flowing over the curved top of the wing has to move further and faster than the air flowing underneath. The greater pressure of the slower air (under the wing) pushes the plane up.

DRAG: the air's resistance to the moving object.

THRUST: produced by the engine propeller.

WEIGHT: the force of gravity pulls the plane downwards.

Controlling the plane

In the air, a plane can roll (from left to right), pitch (up and down) as well as turn.

The pilot uses the control stick to change roll (A) or pitch (B), and the rudder pedals to turn the aircraft (C).

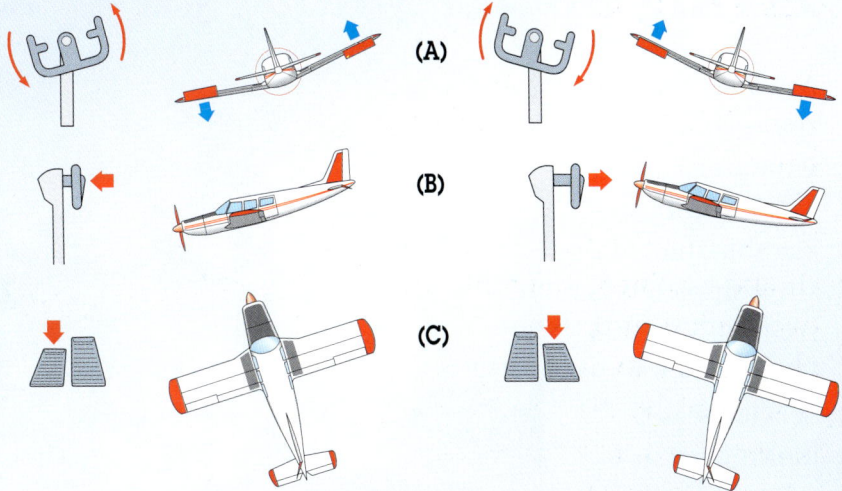

(A)

(B)

(C)

Getting the balance right

1. Taking off: Opening the throttle makes the plane go faster. Air moves faster over the wings, this increases lift and the plane rises.

2. In flight: To increase speed and keep the plane at a steady height, the pilot lowers the nose slightly when opening the throttle. This stops the plane from rising further.

After the necessary hours of flying practice, Mwanza was ready to make her first solo flight.

❝It was great, the aircraft felt so light. As soon as I lifted off, I pushed the back of the instructor's chair down, just to make sure I was really on my own! After circling the airfield, and landing correctly, I was able to fly cross-country, either on my own or with another student. It was great fun and helped to build my confidence.❞

However, things did not all run smoothly. Due to technical problems, the student pilots experienced a number of delays in their training, and the course lasted a lot longer than the usual eighteen months.

❝This was discouraging, but I was determined not to give up. It was in fact four years before I was able to collect my Commercial Pilot's Licence. They were four long years, but it was worth it.❞

Flying doctor pilot

Mwanza was only the second woman to qualify as a pilot in Zambia. Just after she completed her training, Zambia's Flying Doctor Service was looking for new pilots. Mwanza travelled to Ndola to the Service's headquarters for an interview.

Mwanza talks to the clinic officer (right) and three WorldVision staff who helped to improve a remote rural clinic so that it can be used by the Zambia Flying Doctor Service.

❝Not every newly qualified pilot gets a job right away. And for me this job was a wonderful opportunity. I could use my training to help people in need. I felt very blessed.❞

Mwanza moved from Lusaka to Ndola to join Zambia's Flying Doctor Service team. She soon got to know the rest of the team: as well as the medical staff, there were five other pilots, and a number of workers who had important jobs to do on the ground.

Did you know?

The first flying doctor service began in Australia in 1928. Its main aim was to bring medical help to people living deep in the interior of the country. It made good use of two inventions which were quite new at the time: the radio (communication) and the aeroplane (transport).

Today, there are flying doctor services in Africa, Asia, and in North and South America – in fact in very many places where a doctor needs to reach patients in remote areas, very far from towns and main roads.

The flying doctor service provides:
- emergency air ambulance transport to the nearest hospital
- on-the-spot medical treatment
- health care for rural communities

What do they do?

These **ground staff** are every bit as important as the pilots, if the service is to run properly.

The **flight dispatcher** organises the timetable, or duty roster, for the pilots, so they know when they have to report for duty.

The **radio operator** receives messages from the stations up-country, and quickly informs the duty pilots and medical staff of any emergency.

The **engineer** checks all the planes and repairs them if necessary, to make sure they are in good flying condition. After every flight, the pilot must report any problem they experienced with their aircraft, however small.

Mwanza often flew to three or four of the 32 up-country stations in a day – a round trip of some-times more than 1,000 kilometres – in a Britten Norman Islander with oxygen and other medical supplies. This aircraft can carry up to three people on stretchers and has seats for nine passengers. It is very good for taking off from a short runway. So it is ideal for small rural landing strips.

"A regular part of my job was to take a doctor and a community nurse to different centres. While the doctor treated sick people, the nurse gave children polio injections and ran a clinic giving advice on general health. Visiting these remote centres was an education for me, especially as I had grown up in the city. I learnt a whole lot more about my country and its people."

Emergency!

Over the next five and a half years, Mwanza flew more than 1,000 missions for Zambia's Flying Doctor Service. As well as the routine flights, there was quite a lot of emergency work. Mwanza had to face some unusual and difficult situations.

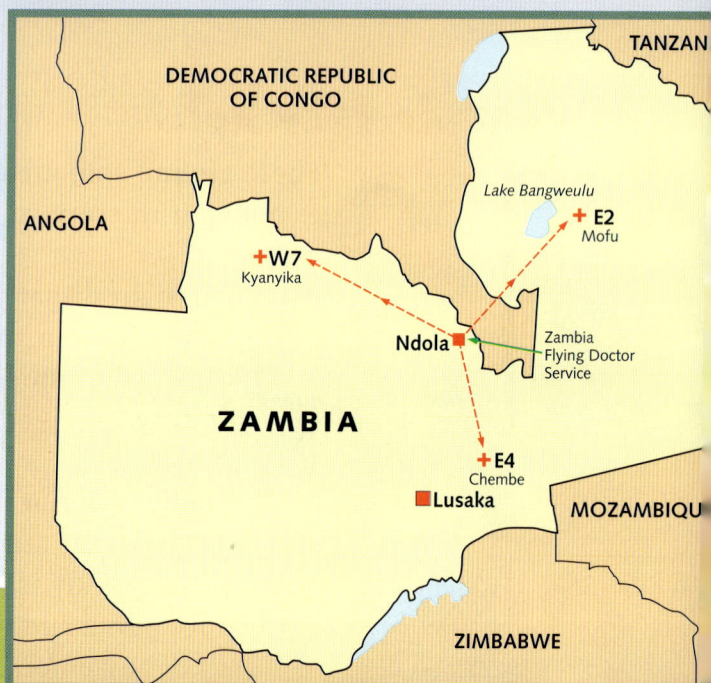

A tragic accident...

"I was still fairly new to the service when we were called out on an emergency – a very bad road accident near Mofu, on the edge of the Bangweulu swamps. I flew the medical team to the nearest station. A man on a motorcycle had been in a head-on crash with a big Land Cruiser and he was very badly injured. The station ground staff brought him on a stretcher and the doctor and nurse helped him into the plane. They did everything they could to save his life, but he died just before we took off. We all had a deep sense of sadness as we flew back to Ndola. Ordinary flight training can't prepare you for this, but you have to keep going. If you are on duty, you might be called to another emergency right away."

Crocodile attack!

❝I remember it was late in the day when the radio message came through. A man was fishing in the river at Chembe (E4) station, about 50 minutes away by air. He'd been bitten by a crocodile and he needed help quickly. We rushed to the aircraft – we needed to get to the man before nightfall, because it's illegal to land on an unlit strip after dark. As soon as we landed, I shut down the engines and the medical team got him into the plane. I restarted the engines and we took off. I thought the worst part was over, but we hit some bad weather on the way back. I knew everyone was depending on me – but they were nervous because the plane was bumping around in the dark. It was a difficult flight and I said a little prayer of thanks when I saw the city lights of Ndola. We made a safe landing and our patient was taken straight to hospital where he made a good recovery.❞

Born in the air!

When Mwanza flew to station W7, she knew she was on her way to help a mother in trouble. Alice Mweshi had just given birth to a baby and there were complications. The officer at the station was worried when he called in on the radio.

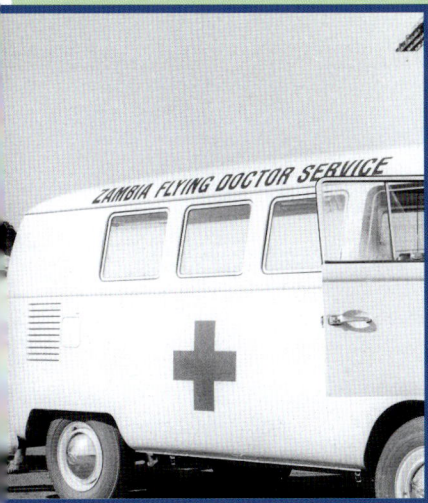

❝After we took off with Alice, there was a lot of excitement in the back of the plane. I couldn't make out what was going on, but after a while the nurse leant forward into the cockpit and asked me to turn back. I must have looked puzzled, so she explained: Alice had given birth to not just one, but two more babies in mid-flight – everything was fine, so we just took her home – we had two extra passengers when we landed!❞

13

Off to the USA

Although she valued her work with the Zambia Flying Doctor Service, Mwanza also wanted to develop her career as a pilot. She wanted to fly bigger planes, so she decided to apply for a job with a passenger airline.

❝It was a difficult decision – I was now married and I had a baby son. Flying commercially would mean longer flights and more time away from home. But I thought, if I don't do this now, I never will. My husband was very supportive, and we made plans together.❞

Eventually Mwanza got her opportunity. She joined an airline company, based in Lusaka. She moved back to the capital city with her family.

❝The first step was a big one. The company sent me to the United States for special training. So for once, I was a passenger in the plane, on my longest air journey so far!❞

In Kansas, USA, Mwanza completed a six-week training course for flying turbine propeller aeroplanes.

The Beech Memorial in Wichita, Kansas. It honours the two founders of the Beechcraft company.

Factfile

Simulators like these are used in many different kinds of flight training, including spacecraft.

The world's big airlines often have their own flight simulator machines. These are based on the type of aircraft used by the airline.

She used a special machine called a flight simulator.

❝In a flight simulator you work the flight controls with a partner and take it in turns to be Captain or First Officer. The instructors give you different emergency situations such as engine failure after take-off, engine fire in flight, electricity or landing gear failures. It feels as if you are in a real aircraft, because the simulator moves like a plane, and you see the sky, mountains or runway on a screen in front of you – it's just like the real thing!❞

❝The simulator is very helpful because it allows for mistakes when you are learning, unlike a real aircraft. If you're not happy about something, you can do it again and again until you are fully confident.❞

Did you know?

When pilots talk to ground staff over the radio, they use this special international alphabet to say the letters that are painted on their aircraft. This identifies the plane they are flying.

A – Alpha	F – Foxtrot	K – Kilo	P – Papa	U – Uniform	Z – Zulu
B – Bravo	G – Golf	L – Lima	Q – Quebec	V – Victor	
C – Charlie	H – Hotel	M – Mike	R – Rome	W – Whisky	
D – Delta	I – India	N – November	S – Sierra	X – X-ray	
E – Echo	J – Juliet	O – Oscar	T – Tango	Y – Yankee	

First Officer on duty

Mwanza is the only woman pilot in a team of ten at the Lusaka-based airline company. What is her day like?

" We have a duty roster for the week, so we each know when to report. All pilots have to report for duty at least forty-five minutes before take-off. My day can start at any time from six o'clock in the morning to five o'clock in the evening, depending on flights. "

Checking the aircraft.

have two officers on the flight: the Captain and First Officer. We can both fly the plane but the Captain gives the orders. This is important because only one person can be in charge of the plane on each flight. You can imagine what a muddle there would be if more than one person was giving instructions! "

Mwanza is going to pilot the plane for take-off to Ndola. She and Captain Chikuye will share the work of planning the flight and flying the aircraft.

First, Mwanza starts the pre-flight checks. She checks the outside of the plane, to make sure that the engine covers are securely shut, and there are no signs of damage to the body of the aircraft. Then she climbs into the plane. She will continue the checks in the cockpit right up to take-off, throughout the flight, and before and after landing.

With the flight crew before an evening flight.

Today, Mwanza is flying as First Officer on the morning flight to Ndola.

" The Beechcraft 1900D that we will fly has seats for 17 passengers and one cabin crew member. We

airspeed indicator – shows how fast the aircraft is going through the air

flight instrument system – these panels give information about the aircraft's horizontal position, and flight direction

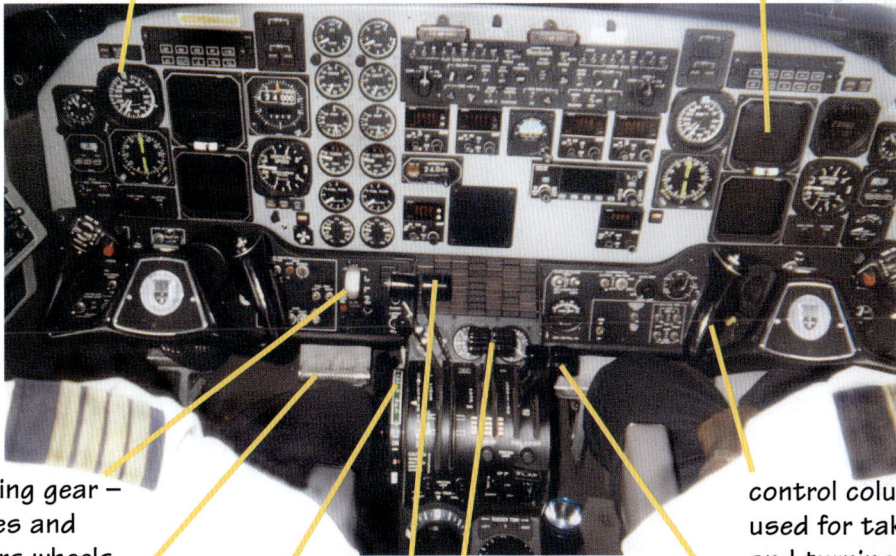

landing gear – raises and lowers wheels

control column (joystick) used for take-off, climbing, and turning or 'banking' the aircraft

pedal for steering the aircraft on the ground, and for braking

controls for the elevators

levers to control angle of propellers for different stages of flight

throttles for engine power

levers to control the amount of fuel to the engine

Departure of Flight 204

The passengers come on board (1). Their luggage is put into the hold – a special compartment at the back of the plane (2). All doors and hatches are closed.

The engines are started, and the propellers begin to turn. On the ground the engineer removes the chock in front of the nose wheel and the plane can move forward (3).

The aircraft taxies towards the runway. Captain Chikuye uses the radio to report to the control tower. The runway is clear and the air traffic controller in the tower gives them permission to take off.

The aircraft heads down the runway (4). It moves faster until it reaches a speed of 100 to 105 knots, then it lifts smoothly into the air, climbing at an angle of 8 to 10 degrees. This is a busy time for Mwanza. She must keep checking her height, angle and speed. At the right moment, the wheels and the wing flaps are raised.

Factfile

- Air traffic controllers direct each and every plane as it takes off or lands. The pilot flies inside an 'air corridor' which is rather like a path in the air. An air corridor is about 6 kilometres wide and is set at a particular height between 1,500 to 12,000 metres. Pilots use the flight instruments to help them fly within these safe corridors.
- Take-off, landing and wind speeds are measured in knots (or nautical miles per hour). A knot is equal to about 1.85 kilometres per hour.

In the Lusaka control tower.

"Once we have reached our cruising level we can relax a bit. If we are going to fly over an interesting landmark, we tell the passengers to watch out for this. It's important to speak clearly and calmly, so that passengers relax and enjoy their flight with us."

The flight descends towards Ndola thirty minutes later. Captain Chikuye talks to air traffic control at Ndola airport, while Mwanza prepares the plane for landing. The aircraft approaches the main runway and lands smoothly.

Captain Chikuye wearing the radio control head-set and safety belt.

Mwanza slows the plane down by changing the angle of the propellers after the aircraft touches the ground. She steers the aircraft slowly to its parking spot, guided by a marshaller with two big round bats. When the engines are shut down, the passengers from Lusaka can leave the plane.

There's only a short stop before the return flight, and then it's back to Lusaka with a new set of passengers. After that, there's the paperwork.

"After each flight I have to make sure that the technical log is completed. The details of every flight are recorded in this special book. It's the pilot's job to see that it's kept up to date for each aircraft they fly."

Factfile

The log includes
- any faults that must be corrected before the aircraft flies again.
- take-off and landing times – every plane has a check by the engineers after 200 hours of flying time.

Customer care

Mwanza is a member of a flight crew. On the Beechcraft 1900D, this is made up of three people:

Captain	First Officer
Cabin crew member	

The passenger cabin is managed by a flight attendant. She explains the flight safety rules to the passengers and looks after them during the flight. She serves drinks and snacks, and gives help to anyone who needs it. She makes sure that everyone is sitting safely at take-off and landing times.

On the ground too, there are members of staff who attend to customers' needs.

Fossie works in the airline office. She deals with all telephone calls, and takes messages. This is an important part of the travel business. People telephone to make reservations, or to meet a flight; someone may want to hire an aeroplane for a special charter, or private flight. Fossie helps all these customers.

Florence does both ground and air duties. She's the cabin crew supervisor and she makes sure that everything in the cabin is in order before departure.

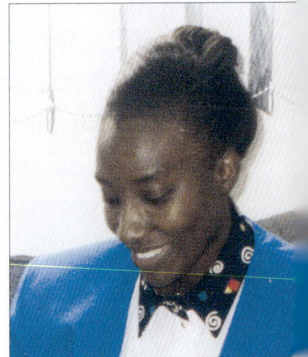

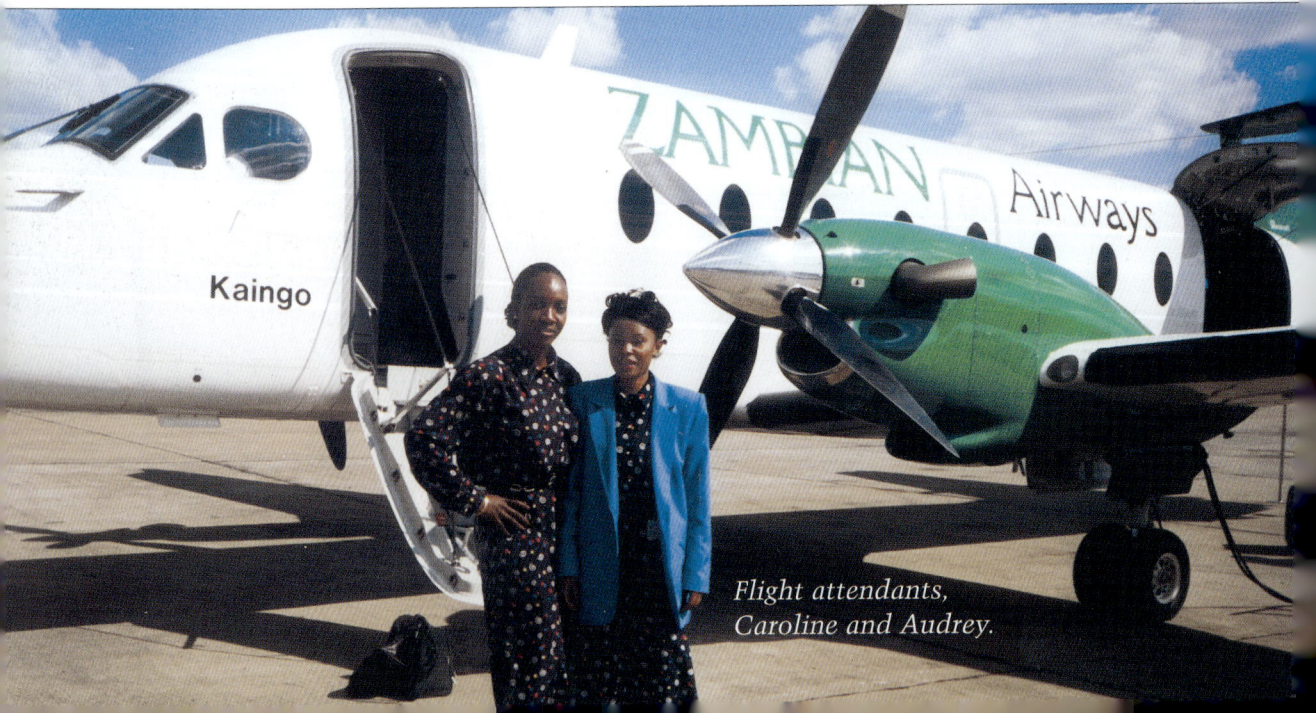

Flight attendants, Caroline and Audrey.

Mwanza on the ground

Mwanza likes to spend her spare time with her husband and son, Mambwe.

❝I enjoy family life. My mother is retired now and she helps to look after Mambwe when I'm away. She helps too if I have a weekend flight or one with an overnight stop, which happens about once a month.❞

Sometimes Mwanza visits schools to talk about her work. Here are some of the questions that young people often ask her.

How high do you fly and how fast?

Planes fly at different heights depending on their design. The usual flying height for smaller passenger planes like ours is about 25,000 feet above sea level. Bigger jet aircraft fly higher – about 37,000 feet. We usually try to fly at a speed of about 270 to 280 knots, that's about 540 kilometres an hour. Like cars, aeroplanes have a steady cruising speed which uses less fuel, so we try to keep to those speeds. However, a lot depends on wind and other weather conditions.

Is it hard to be the only woman pilot?

Well, I think you have to work hard to earn the respect of the other pilots in the team. And as a young pilot you have to be willing to learn from others.

Sometimes you have to explain yourself to passengers, too. One important politician once boarded the plane and asked me: 'Where's the pilot?' He was a bit embarrassed when I told him I was flying the plane! These days, people usually just say: 'Thank you, gentlemen', or: 'Oh sorry, it's a lady!'

Did you have to pay a lot of money for your training?

No. I was on a government course, so most of my training was paid for by the government. There are private flying schools, but private lessons are very expensive. Once you have your basic training, an airline will train you to fly bigger planes. And all pilots must pass regular tests to keep their flying licences.

What's the most beautiful thing you've ever seen from the air?

I sometimes fly tourists to Mfuwe in Zambia's beautiful Luangwa Valley. And then there's the Victoria Falls – from the air these are spectacular. The sunset is also a wonderful thing to see from the air – in the east it's already dark and there's a brilliant sun going down in the west.

Victoria Falls.

Activities

Who's talking?

Choose the correct speaker for each of these sentences:

1 This is Nine Juliet Mike Alpha Sierra. Request landing clearance...

2 Please fasten your seat-belts, ready for take-off.

3 Cleared taxi to holding point runway one zero. Wind zero one zero at five knots...

4 I've replaced the air filter in number two engine...

engineer

pilot

flight attendant

air traffic controller

Complete your pilot's log

You are flying a Beechcraft 1900D. The aircraft is full.

- How many people are there on the plane? Don't forget the flight crew! (*Check on page 16.*)

- The clocks below show your departure and arrival times. How long is the flight?

- You fly five miles in a minute. How many miles will you fly?

- Your two engines each use 400 lb per hour of flying time. How much fuel will they use on this trip?

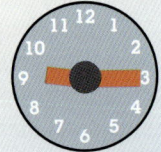

A pilot's puzzle

Can you find the missing words to complete the sentences?
(*For extra clues see pages 8–9 and 15.*)

When a pilot flies on her own, she flies   ☐ _ L _ .

Alpha is radio code for the letter   ☐ .

Lift, weight, thrust and drag are all   ☐ _ R C _ S .

These help the aircraft to climb: ☐ L _ V _ T _ R S .

A pilot uses this to control engine power: ☐ _ _ _ _ T L _ .

Does Mwanza enjoy flying?   ☐ _ _ !

What is the most important part of flying?
The letters in the boxes should spell the answer.